The Bible on DIVORCE and REMARRIAGE

Michael Pearl

International best-selling author of GOOD AND EVIL

Publication date: October 2015

Print: ISBN: 978-1-61644-079-4
ePub: ISBN: 978-1-61644-080-0
ePDF: ISBN: 978-1-61644-081-7

All Scripture quotations are taken from the King James Holy Bible

Library of Congress Control Number: 2015914719

This publication is designed to provide accurate and authoritative information in regard to the subject matter covered. It is sold with the understanding that the author or the publisher is not engaged in rendering any type of professional services. If expert assistance is required, the services of a competent professional should be sought.

1. Marriage 2. Divorce 3. Remarriage 4. Counseling 5. Religion 6. Scripture 7. Bible 8. Christianity
I. Pearl, Michael II. The Bible on Divorce and Remarriage

The Bible on Divorce and Remarriage may be purchased at special quantity discounts for churches, donor programs, fund raising, book clubs, or educational purposes for churches, congregations, schools and universities. Rights and Licensing in other languages and international sales opportunities are available. For more information contact:

Mel Cohen
1000 Pearl Road
Pleasantville TN 37033
(931) 593-2484
mcohen@nogreaterjoy.org

Cover design by Megan Van Vuren
Interior layout by Michael Pearl and Aaron Aprile
Printed in the United States of America

Publisher: No Greater Joy Ministries, Inc.
www.nogreaterjoy.org

Introduction

Ten Months in Separate Bedrooms

Dear Mr. Pearl,

One day I began to pray for God to open my eyes to His truth and not let me continue to believe any false doctrines or lies. To my surprise, I was convicted right away in the area of my "marriage" of 12+ years. We are both divorced from spouses and now have two children together. I was divorced twice before I was 22 years old.

In the last year, whenever I have asked God for confirmation, I have been consistently and repeatedly convicted from Scripture about the issue: we should never have married, and are, in truth, adulterers; so for ten months we have lived together in separate bedrooms.

Our church does not agree with my conviction, and many in our church as well as other Christian leaders have admonished me that we should resume our lives as "married."

The Scriptures used by different "churches" to support a remarriage after divorce are vague. But the Scriptures against remarriage after divorce are not even slightly vague; they are clear and concise.

While reading your material on parenting, I come across your marriage stuff and it stirs deep feelings about marriage. Otherwise I have done well suppressing any "wife" feelings. Usually I pray that God will remove unclean thoughts and feelings from me, and I don't think about the marriage part much at all. Of course there is stress, tension . . . well, I am sure you can guess this is not smooth sailing.

I am wondering if you are willing to offer me a glass full of that vinegar you specialize in (AKA: your thoughts in terms most sane people would shy away from using) because for some reason I feel compelled to ask for it.

— From a reader

Well, you did ask, so I have written a book to answer your question and a thousand other letters like yours that we have received over the years. Your husband will appreciate it, and from what you say of your "deep feelings" you are trying to "suppress," I think you will appreciate it as well.

Foreword

My views on marriage, divorce, and remarriage have remained the same for the past fifty years, ever since I first studied the Scriptures in a serious manner. My audio messages on 1 Corinthians, published many years ago, express the same views as those found in this book.

In writing many books and magazine articles covering just about every Bible subject, I have avoided writing on the subject of divorce and remarriage. I am not sure why. Possibly because it is such an uncomfortable subject. But the time has come.

There are many books written that come to the same conclusions as does this one, so why write another? I have yet to read a book or online article that satisfactorily addresses all the Scripture on the subject. So I do think I have something fresh to contribute to the issue. May the spirit of grace and peace rest upon those who need a biblical answer to the awful question, "Can I remarry without sinning?"

Table of Contents

" *Wherefore they are <u>no more</u> twain,
but* **one flesh**. *
What therefore God hath*
joined *together,
let <u>not</u> man put asunder.* "

Matthew 19:6

Chapter 1

The Bible on Divorce and Remarriage

Historically, Christians have been divided on the issue of divorce and remarriage, many institutions and theologies coming down on the side that it is adultery to remarry while one's former spouse is still alive. This is consistent with the words of Jesus in Matthew 5:32 and 19:9, and the words of the Apostle Paul in Romans 7:1–3. Others stand by the words of Paul in 1 Corinthians 7:15 and 27–28 where he clearly declares that it is not a sin to marry again if you were "put away" (abandoned or divorced) by an unbelieving spouse.

There seems to be a conflict in Scripture regarding divorce and remarriage. In the beginning God established the order of marriage—one man and one woman as long as they both live (Matthew 19:4–6), no exceptions mentioned. Yet the Law of Moses clearly permits the man to divorce his wife and remarry simply because she finds "no favour in his eyes" or he "hates her" (Deuteronomy 24:1–3). In contradiction to the Law, Jesus declares that the only reason one can divorce and remarry is in response to adultery. But then the Apostle Paul asserts that one may remarry if s/he is "put away" (abandoned, divorced) by one's unbelieving partner—again adding a condition of permission that Jesus did not mention.

It is no wonder the church has been divided on this issue. Many have taken what they believe is the higher road, giving more weight to the words of Christ than to the Law of Moses or the dictates of the Apostle Paul. Paul bolstered his revision of both the Law and the words of Christ by saying his view was based on the "Spirit of God" (1 Corinthians 7:40). Paul "ordained" this remarriage doctrine "in all churches" (1 Corinthians 7:17).

Most Christians who find themselves in a divorced state do remarry, but they do so with a measure of guilt and a sense of being out of the will of God. They are not able to justify their remarriage from Scripture. This work should remedy that gap in biblical knowledge.

Reconciling the "Contradictions"

So we have Moses granting divorce even though it is contrary to creation. Then Christ contradicts Moses, and finally Paul contradicts both the Law and Christ. How do we reconcile the contradictions? By believing that all the words of God are inspired and carry equal weight, and then "rightly dividing the word of truth" (2 Timothy 2:15).

This principle of dispensational variations is not new to theologians and Bible students. God commanded the absolute keeping of the Sabbath for Israel, with a death penalty for violation (Numbers 15:32–36). The death penalty was also to be enforced for adultery and homosexual activity, but the church is under no such mandate. God declared certain meats unclean in the Old Testament (Leviticus 11), but then told Peter that he had cleansed all meat and nothing was to be considered unclean (Acts 10:12–15). The same reversal is seen on issues like circumcision, eye for an eye, oaths, and others. In the Old Testament God was silent on the issues of polygamy, concubines, and slavery, yet the New Testament gives clear instruction regarding these topics. God is not fickle. His revelations sometimes accommodate the ability of men to understand and receive his words (Matthew 19:11–12).

The careful Bible student also understands that the Word of God must be rightly divided (2 Timothy 2:15) into its different dispensations if it is to be correctly understood. An ordinance in one dispensation (i.e., circumcision, blood sacrifices, feast days, Sabbath keeping, tithing, etc.) is not necessarily binding in another.

What Is Biblical Marriage?

By nature, marriage is between one man and one woman until death.

Matthew 19:4–6

4 And he answered and said unto them, Have ye not read, that he which made them at the beginning made them male and female,

5 And said, For this cause shall a man leave father and mother, and shall cleave to his wife: and they twain shall be one flesh?

6 Wherefore they are no more twain, but one flesh. What therefore God hath joined together, let not man put asunder.

In the above statement on the pure nature of marriage, Jesus does not mention the exception of adultery because God's original intent was that there would be no fornication or adultery, and therefore no exception to the permanence of marriage. However, given the realities of fallen man, conditions did arise that necessitated exceptions, which God recognizes and regulates. Those exceptions have varied in different dispensations. We will review the development of the divorce and remarriage doctrine from creation to the Apostle Paul.

Holy Matrimony versus State Marriage

Until we have a clear understanding of what constitutes marriage, we cannot understand the nature of divorce. Most people have accepted the legal (state) definition of marriage and are unaware of the biblical doctrine. The concept of obtaining a marriage license from the state is an invention of modern times. It cedes jurisdiction to the state over something that is of divine origin. Ministers officiating at weddings say, "What God hath joined together," acknowledging that holy matrimony is a divine institution that preceded the Law and the gospel, beginning at creation. The state does not do God's work of joining them together. The minister does not do God's work of joining them together. Copulation (an act of man) joins them into *one flesh*, no matter the ceremony or lack thereof. But *holy matrimony* (a work of God) is a <u>combination</u> of a public covenant and a private joining of two bodies.

Ministers make a mistake when they conclude a wedding by saying, "By the **authority vested in me by the state** of Tennessee, I now pronounce you husband and wife." And they usually follow with the statement, "What God therefore hath joined together, let not man put asunder." It is as if the authority rests with the state and God complies. At the very least, ministers should separate the state marriage contract from the church covenant of holy matrimony.

The First Wedding

In the first wedding God gave the bride away, and the groom performed his own marriage, prophesying as he did so, proclaiming the nature of marriage.

Genesis 2:22–24

22 And the rib, which the LORD God had taken from man, made he a woman, and brought her unto the man.

*23 And **Adam said**, This is now bone of my bones, and flesh of my flesh: she shall be called Woman, because she was taken out of Man.*

24 Therefore shall a man leave his father and his mother, and shall cleave unto his wife: and they shall be one flesh.

Jesus Quotes Adam in Support of His Statement about Marriage

Matthew 19:5–6

*5 And said, For this cause shall a man leave father and mother, and shall **cleave** to his wife: and they twain shall be **one flesh**?*

6 Wherefore they are no more twain, but one flesh. What therefore God hath joined together, let not man put asunder.

Jesus tells us that marriage is a man leaving his father and mother and *cleaving* unto his wife as they become one flesh. He elevates the act by recognizing God as the authority behind the one-flesh union that is the essence of marriage.

The man **cleaves** unto his wife. To cleave is to open up and divide without severing (Leviticus 1:17), and it also carries the meaning of "cling to" or "adhere to." A man cleaves his wife in the sexual union, and as he *parts* and *adheres to*, they become one flesh—"bone of my bones, and flesh of my flesh."

Marriage Ceremonies

Down through history there have been diverse cultural expressions to formalize and celebrate a marriage, ranging from jumping over a broom together to copulating in a bed, behind a veil and under covers, with family watching to make sure the marriage is consummated and that the woman bleeds to demonstrate her virginity.

In all cultures, the difference between fornication and marriage is the public declaration made by the couple. A public covenant is universally considered to be a necessary precursor to the one-flesh union.

A minister or justice of the peace is not essential to the creation of holy matrimony. Holy matrimony is a culturally appropriate covenant between a man and a woman performed in public.

The state cannot conduct holy matrimony for anyone. But it can license a marriage between two sodomites performed by an Elvis Presley impersonator in a motel room in Las Vegas.

The Marriage of Isaac to Rebekah Was without Ceremony

Genesis 24:67

And Isaac brought her into his mother Sarah's tent, and took Rebekah, and she became his wife; and he loved her: and Isaac was comforted after his mother's death.

The servant had traveled to a far place to acquire a bride for Isaac. Upon meeting her, Isaac, in front of the family and servants, took her into his deceased mother's tent, and "loved her." That, along with the general public knowledge that she was to be his wife, was a culturally appropriate commencement to a lifelong union. And in the tent as they availed themselves of the divine gift of sexual union (Isaac "cleaved" unto his wife) they entered the designation of being joined together by God.

The Difference between Fornication and Marriage

A sexual relationship without making a binding public commitment is not *marriage*. It does join two people into a *one-flesh union*, but it is still fornication. When Jesus confronted the woman at the well, he declared, "For thou hast had five husbands; and he whom thou now hast is not thy husband . . ." (John 4:18). He made a distinction between being married—probably divorced and remarried several times—and just shacking up. Apparently the woman was in a relationship with a man to whom she had not made a public commitment. In an era when common law marriages were common, if you had asked the people in the city if the woman was married, they would have said, "No, but she is living with a man right now." The woman had reached that point in a troubled life filled with disappointment where she did not want to make a binding commitment to any man—at least not to this one, so she enjoyed the benefits of a man without assuming responsibility for a lasting marriage union. That is fornication, and it is an ongoing sin, remedied only by ceasing the relationship or entering into a public covenant.

There was a time when the constraints of the church and the community guaranteed permanent recognition of a marriage. All that was needed was for the minister to pronounce them husband and wife and for them or their parents to record it in the family Bible. But due to the loss of community and the complexities of the legal structure, it is not that simple today. So apart from a signed marriage license provided by the state, the best safeguard to assure your rights as a spouse is a signed covenant of marriage drawn up by an attorney and filed at the courthouse.

Your state may not recognize what they call "common law marriage," but then we shouldn't recognize their outlaw marriages either. If a private covenant spells out legal responsibilities and privileges, property sharing, children, etc., it must be honored as a legal contract if not as a marriage. After all, the courts do recognize and honor prenuptial agreements or business partnerships. You don't need a government license to enter holy matrimony, but with the possibility of adverse circumstances arising, you may need a contract to navigate the complexities of marriage in a world controlled by the courts.

"When a man hath taken a wife,
and **married her**,
and it come to pass that
she <u>find no favour</u> in his eyes,
because he hath found
some **uncleanness** in her:
then let him write her a
bill of divorcement,
and give it in her hand,
and send her <u>out</u> of his house."

Deuteronomy 24:1

Chapter 2

God Allowed Moses to Grant Divorce and Remarriage for Any Reason

We have surveyed the nature of marriage, God's original design. Now we are going to examine the Law of Moses that permits divorce and remarriage for any reason.

Deuteronomy 24:1–3

*1 When a man hath taken a wife, and married her, and it come to pass that she **find no favour in his eyes**, because he hath found **some uncleanness** in her: then let him write her a bill of divorcement, and give it in her hand, and send her out of his house.*

*2 And when she is departed out of his house, **she may go and be another man's wife**.*

*3 And if the latter husband **hate her**, and write her a bill of divorcement, and giveth it in her hand, and sendeth her out of his house . . .*

Some have suggested that the term "some uncleanness" is referring to fornication prior to their marriage, but that cannot be the case for two reasons. One, if fornication is what the writer meant, he would have said so. Secondly, if she was proven to be guilty of fornication prior to the marriage, he would not have needed to divorce her, for she would have suffered the death penalty under the Law (Deuteronomy 22:20–22).

To give weight to the interpretation that Moses was granting divorce for every cause is the statement in verse 3 that the second husband could put her away if he comes to "hate her." Hate is hate, not fornication.

Furthermore, the words of Moses can best be understood through the minds of the Jews who spoke the Hebrew language and had the benefit of a historical understanding of the text. They understood the words of Moses to grant divorce "for every cause."

Matthew 19:3

*The Pharisees also came unto him, tempting him, and saying unto him, Is it lawful for a man to put away his wife for **every cause**?*

The Pharisees, knowing the narrow position Jesus had been espousing earlier (in Matthew 5), were tempting him to state it now, in their presence, so they could accuse him of contradicting the Law of Moses.

Allowing divorce is not the same as condoning it. The Jews provoked God by taking advantage of this liberal policy regarding divorce and remarriage.

Malachi 2:16

For the LORD, the God of Israel, saith that he hateth putting away: for one covereth violence with his garment, saith the LORD of hosts: therefore take heed to your spirit, that ye deal not treacherously.

Rabbi Hillel taught that "a man may divorce his wife even if she burned his soup . . . or spoiled a dish for him." Rabbi Akiva taught that divorce was acceptable "if he should find a woman fairer than his wife." Other rabbis, sensing the injustice and ungodliness of it all, took the liberty to place more restrictions on divorce.

Though God allowed Moses to permit divorce and remarriage, he rebuked them for their treacherous spirit in regard to divorce. Human nature is such that if you make an allowance, selfish souls will seize it with gusto.

Moses Provided One Exception to Remarriage

Deuteronomy 24:3–4

3 And if the latter husband hate her, and write her a bill of divorcement, and giveth it in her hand, and sendeth her out of his house; or if the latter husband die, which took her to be his wife;

*4 Her **former husband, which sent her away, may not take her again to be his wife**, after that she is defiled; for that is **abomination** before the LORD: and thou shalt not cause the land to* *sin, which the LORD thy God giveth thee for an inheritance.*

This law was apparently written to prevent hasty divorce and humiliation of the woman. Men could not use women as a swinging door—mine today, yours tomorrow, then mine again. This verse is ignored by the cult-like groups that encourage a remarried woman to leave her second husband and children and return to her first husband. To do so would be an "abomination before the LORD." If either of them have ever remarried, they cannot under any circumstances reconstitute their marriage to each other.

Why Would God Allow Divorce and Remarriage When It Is Contrary to the Created Order?

The question as to why God would publish a law that allowed remarriage after putting away a spouse is answered by Jesus in Matthew 19, which we will examine next.

Chapter 3

Jesus Reveals a Position Different from Creation and Radically Different from the Law

The nineteenth chapter of Matthew is most pertinent to the doctrine of divorce and remarriage. The individual parts are best understood in context, so I have provided a commentary on that portion of Scripture dealing with our subject.

Matthew 19:3–12

3 The Pharisees also came unto him, tempting him, and saying unto him, Is it lawful for a man to put away his wife for every cause?

The Pharisees reflect the view of the majority of the Jews—that a man could indeed put away his wife for any reason. They are well aware that Jesus had made statements about the singularity of marriage, and they are aware that his view is contrary to the Law of Moses and the sentiment of the people, so they seek to entrap him into affirming a rejection of their most sacred Law. Such a narrow view would cause many to reject Jesus, which was their end game. Even his disciples had trouble with his answer (19:10), indicating it was a radical departure from their former practice and understanding.

> *4 And he answered and said unto them,* **Have ye not read,** *that he which made them* **at the beginning** *made them male and female,*

With this rhetorical question, "Have ye not read?" Jesus exposes their failure to pay attention to the words of God. Of course they have read, but they are acting as if they haven't. Jesus knows the game of entrapment is on, and before he answers them, he prepares the ground by reframing the issue; it is not an issue of what Moses reluctantly allowed, but of what God originally intended. "The beginning" comes before Moses and must be afforded due respect.

> *5 And said, For this cause shall a man leave father and mother, and shall cleave to his wife: and they twain shall be one flesh?*
>
> *6 Wherefore they are no more twain, but one flesh. What therefore God hath joined together, let not man put asunder.*

That quote of Adam, "What therefore God hath joined together, let not man put asunder," has made it more difficult for them to ask the question they are about to spring on him.

> *7 They say unto him,* **Why did Moses then command to give a writing of divorcement, and to put her away?**

They have the support of the Law of Moses—Deuteronomy 24:1–4. This is their "gotcha" moment. In their ignorance they think he takes the bait by stating a position contrary to the Law of Moses.

> *8 He saith unto them, Moses because of the* **hardness of your hearts** <u>*suffered*</u> *you to put away your wives: but* **from the beginning it was not so.**

Jesus admits that the Law of Moses and God's original intent are different, and he gives the reason—because of the **"hardness of your hearts."**

Suffered

Note the word *suffered*. Moses **suffered** them to put away their wives, constrained to do so because of their fallen condition—hardness of heart.

The word *suffer*, in English as well as Middle English, Old French, Old Latin, and all the way back to the Greek, carries the meaning of allowing something to occur with some degree of trepidation or discomfort or loss to one's self. The dictionary defines it as: "to tolerate, endure pain or evil to one's self." A good example is the use Christ made of it when he rebuked the disciples for preventing the children's access to him. He said, "Suffer little children, and forbid them not, to come unto me . . ." (Matthew 19:14). They found it inconvenient to allow little children to crowd around Christ, preventing the adults from unhindered interaction; so knowing how it pained them, Jesus said, "suffer little children . . ."

The same word is used in Mark 8:31, "And he began to teach them, that the Son of man must **suffer** many things, and be rejected of the elders, and of the chief priests, and scribes, and be killed, and after three days rise again."

As Christ suffered bad things to happen to him, so he suffered men and women with hard hearts to divorce and remarry. He didn't like it. In fact, he hated it (Hebrews 12:2). It was painful to Moses and to God to see the results of hard hearts that ended something God himself had joined together, but Moses was constrained to "suffer" it by a necessity arising from the condition of fallen man.

Men and women are created to live in intimacy with the opposite sex. That powerful fact of human nature cannot be effectively sublimated by most people, so God allowed Moses to suffer remarriage.

Commercial translations that change the word *suffer* to *allow* do indeed strip away the connotation of a word that has no equal in the Indo-European languages, and they are going against nearly 2,000 years of precedence established in the Received Text.

*9 And **I say unto you**, Whosoever shall put away his wife, **except it be for fornication**, and shall marry another, committeth **adultery**: and whoso marrieth her which is put away doth commit **adultery**.*

In effect, Jesus says, "Yes, Moses granted divorce and remarriage for every cause, but 'I say unto you . . .'" asserting his own authority above the Law of Moses.

Jesus does provide for one exception to the permanence of a marriage covenant—fornication, which encompasses all manner of sexual deviancy, including adultery. So he differs with the Law of Moses and he differs with creation where there was no exception.

Rather than squirm his way out of this like a politician, Jesus doubles down on his revision of the law of marriage, affirming God's original intent regarding its permanence.

10 His disciples say unto him, If the case of the man be so with his wife, it is not good to marry.

The disciples had the exact same reaction as many today—in that case it is preferable to cohabitate without the shackles of a marriage gone bad.

11 But he said unto them, All men cannot receive this saying, save they to whom it is given.

It seems he is acknowledging that his position is a high one with limited application, something most people "cannot receive." And in the next verse, he acknowledges that some are not "able to receive it."

*12 For there are some eunuchs, which were so born from their mother's womb: and there are some eunuchs, which were made eunuchs of men: and there be eunuchs, which have made themselves eunuchs for the kingdom of heaven's sake. **He that is able to receive it**, let him receive it.*

The word *eunuch* is not limited to a castrated man or to one who is born physically impaired so as to have no interest in females. It includes all who for whatever reason are in a state of celibacy. Just as the Apostle Paul says it is better not to marry so as to attend to the things of God without distraction (1 Corinthians 7), Christ says that a celibate man is better able to attend to the kingdom of heaven. The 144,000 young Jewish males who will preach the gospel of the kingdom during the tribulation will all be unentangled with women (Revelation 14:4) so they can preach without distraction until their martyrdom.

Paul Is in Agreement with Christ on the Indissolubleness of Marriage according to Nature

Romans 7:1–3

1 Know ye not, brethren, (for I speak to them that know the law,) how that the law hath dominion over a man as long as he liveth?

2 For the woman which hath an husband is bound by the law [law of marriage, not the Law of Moses] to her husband so long as he liveth; but if the husband be dead, she is loosed from the law of her husband.

3 So then if, while her husband liveth, she be married to another man, she shall be called an adulteress: but if her husband be dead, she is free from that law; so that she is no adulteress, though she be married to another man.

Paul uses the law of marriage (not the Law of Moses) to illustrate how the sinner is wed to his flesh, and how the flesh (former husband) must die in order to gain the freedom to become one with Christ (a new husband). The illustration depends upon an immutable law that can only be escaped by death. So in this passage Paul agrees with Christ in Matthew 19:4–6, where he provided no exception—that marriage is until death.

The Reason Adultery Dissolves the Marriage

The reason adultery dissolves the marriage covenant is not because it is so offensive to the innocent party that it gives him/her reason to abandon the covenant. Rather, it is that the act of adultery itself dissolves the marriage covenant. In verses 5–6, above, Jesus describes the nature of marriage as the merging of two bodies in the act of copulation so that "they are no more twain, but one flesh." Jesus instructs us not to "put asunder" what he joined together for the very reason that a man **can** indeed "put asunder" his marriage by breaking the one-flesh union in the act of adultery.

Dealing with this subject, Paul says, "What? know ye not that he which is joined to an harlot is one body? **for two**, saith he, **shall be one flesh**" (1 Corinthians 6:16). Paul defines the union with a harlot as consummating into "one flesh," quoting the passage in Genesis that pertained to the original union of Adam and Eve, "and they shall be one flesh" (Genesis 2:24). Without question when a married man takes a harlot, he becomes one flesh with her and breaks the former union with his covenant wife. The adulterous man has "put away" his wife by means of the act of adultery. According to Jesus, she is then free to go and marry another man. The wife, in publicly putting away her husband for reason of adultery, is simply formalizing what the adulterous husband did in becoming one flesh with another woman. In our modern era, what we call "divorce" is nothing more than a court proceeding to change one's legal status. In reality, the divorce takes place when one of the parties breaks the one-flesh union, leaving the other free to remarry.

Summary

It is quite clear from this passage that Moses granted a dispensation of exemption from the original intent of God concerning marriage, divorce, and remarriage.

It is also clear that the permissiveness of the Law of Moses regarding divorce and remarriage was something God suffered his prophet to institute due to the extenuating circumstances of fallen humanity. Their hearts were too hard to be faithful to the perfect will of God, so rather than create an entire nation of outlaws, God allowed Moses to permit divorce and remarriage, just as he allowed slavery and polygamy. But where God was simply silent on slavery and polygamy, he actually allowed Moses to canonize remarriage. Jesus reveals that though God *suffered*

divorce and remarriage to take place under Moses'
Law, it was not in accord with his perfect will.

> "Now concerning the things
>   whereof ye wrote unto me:
> It is *good* for a man
>   **not to touch** a woman."
>
> *1 Corinthians 7:1*

Chapter 4

Paul Grants Divorce and Remarriage on Grounds of Putting Away

We have seen the law of marriage change twice since creation. At creation there was no divorce or remarriage for any reason. Then, due to hardened hearts that destroyed marriages, God suffered Moses to direct them to write a bill of divorcement before remarrying. Then Christ went back to the original intention of God but altered it by saying that there is one cause for divorce that allows remarriage—when one is the victim of adultery. Now we come to the Apostle Paul who also suffers divorce and remarriage, as did Moses, but under conditions more restraining than Moses but more liberal than Christ.

Paul, by Permission of the Spirit, Grants Remarriage

1 Corinthians 7:27–28

27 Art thou bound unto a wife? seek not to be loosed. Art thou loosed from a wife? seek not a wife.

28 But and if thou marry, thou hast not sinned; and if a virgin marry, she hath not sinned. Nevertheless such shall have trouble in the flesh: but I spare you.

This passage is part of Paul's letter to the Corinthians. To assure there will be no misunderstanding of the passage, we will look at the context very closely. First, we need to review a little of what we know about the city of Corinth, the place where the church was located.

The City of Corinth

The book of 1 Corinthians was written to the church at Corinth to address a number of problems. Corinth was a city of debauchery. The most prominent deity in Corinth was Aphrodite, the goddess of lust and fertility. An inherent part of her worship was the practice of ritual prostitution in her shrines and temples.

When Paul addressed the church, he noted the makeup of the congregation. They had been fornicators, idolaters, adulterers, effeminate (sodomites), abusers of themselves with mankind, (group bondage and orgies), and more (1 Corinthians 6:9–11). One of the church members was copulating with his stepmother (1 Corinthians 5:1).

The church at Corinth was in a state of "distress" (1 Corinthians 7:26), in part brought on by believers having spouses that were unbelievers. In some cases unbelievers were divorcing their believing spouses. There was confusion as to how believers should relate to their unbelieving spouses. There was also distress in the slave/master relationship and a question of circumcision. And then there was a question of remarriage of a believer who had been put away by an unbelieving spouse. These issues needed to be clarified, so this young church wrote a letter to Paul, asking his advice.

Questions from Corinth

To many, the seventh chapter of 1 Corinthians is a rather directionless and confusing discussion of several subjects that do not appear to be related. The primary subject of marriage seems to be a jumble of God speaking one thing and Paul speaking something else, even contradicting each other. But the chapter makes a lot more sense when you pay attention to the very first verse. Paul is writing to the church "concerning the things whereof ye wrote unto me." He is answering a list of questions posed by the Corinthian church. Paul does not restate the questions. The Corinthians already knew the questions, but since we don't have the benefit of knowing the questions, we must surmise from the answer what the questions might have been. That helps us to better organize the material, and in doing so we discover that it is not random or confusing at all.

Commentary on 1 Corinthians 7

Question:

Now that I am a Christian and my spouse is not, should I leave him, or should I avoid copulating with him until he becomes a believer? Or maybe believers should abstain from marital copulation altogether?

Answer:

I know of several church groups that actually teach that a man and wife should not copulate unless it is an attempt to create a baby. They believe that once women pass the childbearing age they should abstain from sex altogether. Most admit to being backsliders. Understandably so! The problem is that it creates "distress" when one must live under that kind of "bondage" (1 Corinthians 7:15).

> *1 Corinthians 7:1*
>
> *Now concerning the things whereof ye **wrote unto me**: It is good for a man not to touch a woman.*

Note that Paul is answering questions they "wrote unto" him. With the understanding we gather from the rest of the chapter, we know that Paul is granting them permission to not have a wife—to be celibate. But he is also revealing a general principle of male nature. Given the male propensity to be provoked by the touch of a woman, it is good for a man to keep his hands off of the opposite sex. It is the second step to fornication; the first is looking upon (Matthew 5:28).

*2 Nevertheless, to avoid fornication, let **every** **man** have his own wife, and let **every** woman have her own husband.*

These first two verses introduce the subject and are a summary of the entire chapter, as it will deal with the value of not touching a woman—not being married—and it will deal with the need for every man and every woman (including those that had been divorced as well as the virgins) to have a spouse so as to avoid the fornication that was so rampant in Corinth.

There is a principle here that we need to take note of: By nature most men and women have an overwhelming need to share intimacy with a member of the opposite sex. The single state leaves one extremely vulnerable to immorality, so "let every man have his own wife, and let every woman have her own husband."

In answer to the supposed question, "should I abstain from marital relations with my unsaved spouse," Paul writes:

3 Let the husband render unto the wife due benevolence: and likewise also the wife unto the husband.

4 The wife hath not power of her own body, but the husband: and likewise also the husband hath not power of his own body, but the wife.

*5 Defraud ye not one the other, except it be with consent for a time, that ye may give yourselves to fasting and prayer; and come together again, that Satan **tempt you not** for your incontinency.*

Regular sex with one's spouse diminishes temptation. But take note: God created us to be sexual beings, to be motivated by healthy lust. It takes a very unusual man to just sublimate his sexual drive and focus his energies on something creative. The production of semen in a man and the inevitable demand of hormones does the same thing to a man that it does to a bull locked in a pen downwind from a pasture full of cows in heat. It is not a matter of choice. He cannot be "spiritual" enough to prevent the rise of the flesh. The heart can be spiritual but the body is always carnal and cannot be otherwise.

That is why Paul did not address the issue of sexual drive with a command to just cease lusting. Rather he began the chapter with, ". . . to avoid fornication, let every man have his own wife, and let every woman have her own husband (1 Corinthians 7:2). And again he says, "But if they cannot contain, let them marry: for it is better to marry than to burn [with lust]" (1 Corinthians 7:9). He acknowledged, ". . . every man hath his proper gift . . ." (v. 7). And he assumes that the cure for lust is to have a spouse that is regularly available to satisfy one's desires.

Any man by nature is going to have a difficult time being put in proximity to the opposite sex yet denied regular satisfaction. But the believer has an enemy, Satan, who is prepared to tempt us at our most vulnerable point, and when a wife defrauds her husband regular satisfaction, he is prime for sexual temptation.

Dear lady, if you think your husband can just pray and do without, you must think you are married to Christ or the Apostle Paul. Has your husband proven to be the most disciplined and self-denying man you have ever met? Does he strike you as the martyr type? No? Well, has he been castrated? No again? So you now expect him to exercise the most extreme form of human self-denial? If not, then stop defrauding your husband and start pumping him dry about every other day or so. If he is younger than 25, make that every day and twice on Sunday. When he begs for mercy or claims to have a headache, you will know you have met his quota. The key is to be *available* and *willing*.

If you do not cheerfully, joyously make yourself available as a willing participant, you are the tool of Satan to bring your husband down. "The wife hath not power of her own body, but the husband [has power of her body]" (1 Corinthians 7:4).

Sir, your wife also has needs, maybe more than you do. So you need to get your rest, and perform for her as she has need.

Summary of the Answer

It is perfectly permissible to not be married, but marriage is a defense against fornication, so everyone who burns with lust or passion should have a husband or wife and not deny their partner sexual fulfillment.

Permission (Continuing with 1 Corinthians 7)

> 6 But I speak this by permission, and **not of commandment**.

That which Paul is about to say is "not of commandment," that is, it is not found in the commandments of God, nor has God commanded Paul to say it.

Paul encourages the unmarried to remain unmarried, as he is.

> 7 For I would that all men were even as I myself. But every man hath his proper gift of God, one after this manner, and another after that.

The sexual drive is a "gift of God." Men are not created equal in regard to their sexual drive. This finds parallel in what Jesus said in Matthew 19:11 ". . . all men cannot receive this saying . . ." and again in verse 12, "He that is able to receive it, let him receive it."

> 8 **I say** therefore to the unmarried and widows, It is good for them if they abide even as I.

This Paul said by permission.

> 9 But if they cannot contain [contain their sexual drive], let them marry: for it is better to marry than to burn [with lust or passion].

Summary of 7–9

God didn't tell me to say this, but he has permitted me to give my understanding of the matter. I would like to see all unmarried persons remain unmarried even as I, but every man has a different level of sexual drive, so if being unmarried may lead to sexual impurity, then it is better to marry.

Back to the Question:
Should I Put Away My Unbelieving Spouse?

He interrupts his statement of permission with a reaffirmation of God's original intent:

> *10 And unto the married I command, yet **not I, but the Lord**, Let not the wife depart from her husband:*

When Paul says, **"not I, but the Lord,"** he is clearly denoting the difference between God's original intent and the allowance he is making in this dispensation.

> *11 But and if she depart, let her remain unmarried or be reconciled to her husband: and let not the husband put away his wife.*

There is no exception given here, not even adultery, because Paul is restating the unchangeable law of nature—one man/one woman as long as they both shall live, and no remarriage after divorce. This is different from the Law of Moses and different from what he is permitting in this chapter.

Now Paul Reveals the Thing God Has Given Him Permission to Say—Something God Has Previously Not Said

> *12 But to the __rest__ speak I, **not the Lord**:*

Note that in verses 10–11 Paul is recounting what God says, the eternal principle of the nature of marriage; now he makes it very clear that what he is saying is not what God has previously said, as stated in 10–11.

"The rest" to whom he speaks are those other than the ones who abide as he—unmarried—and other than those in verses 10 and 11 who maintained a first marriage.

Take note: If Paul is saying something that required permission because God never said it, then Paul is saying something different from verses 10 and 11, and from Matthew 19, and from the Mosaic Law, and from what he said in Romans 7:1–3.

He will not immediately address his departure from what Christ said. First he lays the groundwork by discussing the divorce that will lead to the question of remarriage. Verse 15 will begin to get to the heart of his Spirit-guided dispensation of remarriage.

12(b) If any brother hath a wife that believeth not, and she be pleased to dwell with him, let him not put her away.

It was the sentiment of the believers in Corinth to put away their unbelieving pagan spouses. He commands them to keep the marriage intact if at all possible.

13 And the woman which hath an husband that believeth not, and if he be pleased to dwell with her, let her not leave him.

Note: In verse 12 he uses the term "put away," and in verse 13 he uses the synonym "leave." Leaving one's spouse and putting one's spouse away are the same thing. One party is the instigator and the other is the victim.

14 For the unbelieving husband is sanctified by the wife, and the unbelieving wife is sanctified by the husband: else were your children unclean; but now are they holy.

Divorce, no matter what the reason, does something to children that is unholy.

In another place Paul tells us that husband and wife are "heirs together of the grace of life" (1 Peter 3:7). When a believer is married to an unbeliever, the unbeliever is in the pipeline for the grace of God, and the children are covered by the covenant relationship of the one believing parent. Divorce deprives the unbelieving spouse of that grace, and the children are left vulnerable as well since they don't have that marital grace unique to couples.

Paul Speaks, Not Christ

So far, from verse 12 through 14, he has not said anything new that would be different from what God commands. The above three verses have been preparation for what he will say next. Now the Apostle Paul is going to give us a new revelation that will differ from the law of marriage as Christ previously stated, and also from what Paul stated in Romans 7.

The New Revelation!

*15 But if the **unbelieving** depart, **let him depart**. A brother or a sister is **not under bondage** ["I spare you" v. 28] in such cases: but God hath called us to peace.*

Many have made the mistake of thinking that Paul has one set of rules for believers and another for unbelievers, and that believers are held to a higher standard. That is not so. The law of marriage precedes both the Mosaic Law and the gospel of Christ and is not altered by one who believes. The same rules apply to all without discrimination.

The phrase, ". . . if the unbelieving depart . . ." carries the assumption that only an unbeliever would choose to break up a marriage. The entire chapter assumes that all believers will hold their marriage vows sacred and not participate in ending the marriage. Only if the marriage is ended against one's will by adultery or desertion (putting away) would a believer or an unbeliever be out from under the "bondage" of a miserable marriage.

The "not under bondage" is the beginning of the new thing he is saying to "the rest." He will expand on it in the following verses as he develops his thoughts.

16 For what knowest thou, O wife, whether thou shalt save thy husband? or how knowest thou, O man, whether thou shalt save thy wife?

Again, we see an assumption that the believer has hope of winning the unbeliever to Christ and would want to pursue that end, even if it means staying in an unhappy marriage. In Corinth the unbelieving spouse would have been a pagan. This admonition to not readily accept being put away by an unbelieving spouse would be consistent with the commandments of the Lord, with the exception that it is offered as an alternative **one should choose for the good that may come of it** rather than an immutable law.

Continue in the State You Were In When You Came to Christ (17–28)

17 But as God hath distributed to every man [sexual drive]*, as the Lord hath called every one, so let him walk. And so ordain I in all churches.*

The phrase "as the Lord hath called every one" is expanded upon in verses 18–28.

As you were when the Lord "called" you, so you should continue—married to a pagan, divorced and remarried, single, divorced and alone, servant, master, circumcised, or uncircumcised, all of which he will discuss.

Circumcision and Slavery

Paul addresses two other questions, circumcision and slavery, (18–24) and uses them to illustrate the bigger issue of continuing in the state you were in when you came to Christ.

Question:

Now that I am a Christian should I get circumcised?

Answer:

> *18 Is any man called being circumcised? let him not become uncircumcised. Is any called in uncircumcision? let him not be circumcised.*

Obviously, a man could not become uncircumcised, so he is expressing a principle.

> *19 Circumcision is nothing, and uncircumcision is nothing, but the keeping of the commandments of God.*

> *20 Let every man abide in the same calling wherein he was called.*

This is a restatement of the principle he is promoting, first mentioned in verse 17, "as the Lord hath called every one, so let him walk."

Question:

Now that I am a believer does that mean that I am free from my legal indebtedness as a servant?

Answer:

> *21 Art thou called being a servant? care not for it: but if thou mayest be made free, use it rather.*

> *22 For he that is called in the Lord, being a servant, is the Lord's freeman: likewise also he that is called, being free, is Christ's servant.*

He seems to be erasing the distinction between a servant and a master.

> *23 Ye are bought with a price; be not ye the servants of men.*

Social Justice

This is an interesting statement Paul has interjected, "be not ye the servants of men." It does not pertain to our subject, but I cannot resist noting it while it is before us. The gospel is always in danger of being tied to political movements or social reforms for the simple reason that some political movements are just while others are not. But Jesus and the apostles avoided becoming social reformers, which is a needful role at various times throughout history, but not for a minister of the gospel. That is not to say that a minister cannot also be a social reformer, but it is not part of his divine calling. Yet the beliefs of the church do indeed form the debate and direct the populace to a just society. Just as God tolerated polygamy in a culture rife with it, he tolerated slavery in a world where every nation practiced it. But the principles of Scripture are fundamentally against polygamy and slavery. So, while not commanding a cessation of slavery, Paul interjects a statement that would alter the thinking of those who routinely accepted it: "Ye are bought with a price; **be not ye the servants of men**."

When radical social reform begins in the political realm, attempting to change well-entrenched societal norms by popular revolt and constraining behavior through laws, the result is often blood in the streets followed by several generations of resentment. If the first-century church had immediately attempted to right social wrongs with a populace revolt, it would have been so opposed as to obscure its message of Christ and redemption. Therefore Paul said:

24 Brethren, let every man, wherein he is called, therein abide with God.

He has repeated this concept three times. It is the theme of the chapter.

He has supported his conclusion that one should abide in the state he was in when he came to Christ—circumcised or not, servant or not, married or not.

Question:

Is it permissible for a virgin to get married?

Answer:

*25 Now concerning virgins I have **no commandment of the Lord**: yet I give **my judgment**, as one that hath obtained mercy of the Lord to be faithful.*

Again, if Paul is not saying something new that differs from what the Law said or what Christ taught, then he would not say that he had "no commandment of the Lord" regarding it.

*26 I suppose therefore that this is good for the **present distress**, I say, that it is good for a man so to be* [so to be a virgin or what he says in verses 27–28, single].

The "present distress" cannot be persecution, for there is no record of the Corinthians suffering persecution at this early point. The entire chapter reveals the nature of the distress: they were distressed over their marital state, as seen by the context and the following statement in verses 27 and 28.

Question:

My wife put me away; may I remarry without sinning? And may a virgin marry me without sinning?

Answer: (The Heart of the Discussion)

This is the point toward which Paul has been steering his readers, preparing them for this one startling departure from the law of marriage as seen in creation and in the Law, and in Christ's teaching, and in Paul's own words in Romans 7. This is the <u>concession God could not personally make because it is beneath his high standards for marriage</u>. Like he did for Moses, God permits Paul to grant a dispensation of exception due to the hardness of hearts that has led to so many broken marriages.

> *27 Art thou bound unto a wife? seek not to be loosed. **Art thou loosed from a wife? seek not a wife.***

This is in accordance with the principle he stated in verses 17, 20, and 24, which he illustrated with circumcision and servitude: abide in the state you were in when you came to Christ.

> *28 **But and if thou marry, thou hast not sinned; and if a virgin marry, she hath not sinned.** Nevertheless such shall have trouble in the flesh:*

*but **I spare you*** ["not under bondage in such cases"].

By permission from God, under the guidance of the Holy Spirit, the Apostle Paul says that a person who came to Christ having been loosed from a wife, or one whose spouse has put him/her away (divorced), should remain in that single state, **"But and if thou marry, thou has not sinned, and if a virgin marry, she hath not sinned."** Paul has given what he thinks is best—to remain unmarried—but affirms that if one does remarry it is not sin. This concept is reflected in the very first two verses of the chapter: "It is good for a man not to touch a woman. Nevertheless to avoid fornication, let every man have his own wife, and let every woman have her own husband." Now we know why Paul has emphasized that what he has to say is not the commandment of the Lord. Guided by the Holy Spirit, he speaks by permission.

When Paul says a virgin who gets married has not sinned, he must be referring to a virgin marrying a man who has been put away, otherwise it would be preposterous to suggest that for a virgin to get married might be sin. No one has ever believed such a thing. So he must be speaking of a virgin marrying under conditions that would normally be viewed as sin—which would be marrying a man who has been put away. This is in accord with the context.

But do note that the virgin is not marrying a man who put away his wife, nor a man that was been put away because of his adultery.

A remarriage after divorce will result in "trouble in the flesh." If a virgin marries a divorced man, she will have troubles also, because of the baggage he brings to the marriage.

Summary of 18–28

Abide in the state you are in when you come to Christ, whether married or unmarried. If you are loosed (divorced), then stay that way. If you are married to an unbeliever, then stay with him unless he puts you away, in which case it is best not to marry again.

But if a divorced person does remarry he does not sin, and if a virgin should marry a man who has been unjustly put away by his wife, she has not sinned.

Two Instances of Divorce and Remarriage Granted

There is no question that in all dispensations divorce is contrary to the will of God. "For the LORD, the God of Israel, saith that he hateth putting away . . ." (Malachi 2:16). But given the reality of the fallen human condition, God has permitted, and even regulates, the administration of divorce and remarriage.

It is telling that in all of the Word of God there are only two instances of a prophet writing something that God did not command him to write. The first time was Moses concerning divorce and remarriage and the second time was Paul on the same subject. It appears that the holy God could not lessen his eternal standards, but due to the hardness of hearts he found it necessary to give permission to his prophets to sanction that which is beneath the dignity of God's perfect will—the necessity being due to the distress brought on by divorce stemming from weak flesh and hard hearts.

The Reason Paul Thinks the Unmarried State Is Best

The one theme carried through the entire chapter has been an assertion that, given the distress in Corinth, it was better for those who were virgins or divorced to remain unmarried, and for those who were married, even to pagans, to remain married. So Paul ends his dissertation where he started it: "It is good for a man not to touch a woman. Nevertheless, to avoid fornication, let every man have his own wife, and let every woman have her own husband." He now sums up his argument for celibacy and expands upon it.

> *29 But this I say, brethren, the **time is short** [until the world passes away]: it remaineth, that both they that have wives be as though they had none;*

The *short time* is not in anticipation of persecution, as some suggest, for in verse 31 he says again, "for the fashion of this world passeth away," indicating he speaks of the ongoing relationship of the believer to the world, not a temporary condition unique to Corinth.

30 And they that weep, as though they wept not; and they that rejoice, as though they rejoiced not; and they that buy, as though they possessed not;

*31 And they that use this world, as not abusing it: for the **fashion of this world passeth away**.*

The "fashion of this world" will not pass away until the millennial reign of Christ upon the earth.

32 But I would have you without carefulness. He that is unmarried careth for the things that belong to the Lord, how he may please the Lord:

This has been true in all dispensations and will remain so.

33 But he that is married careth for the things that are of the world, how he may please his wife.

This is true by nature. Married people have a duty to think of pleasing their spouse first. A man should not neglect his wife or family for the sake of ministry. But an unmarried person can minister fifteen hours a day instead of three or four.

34 There is difference also between a wife and a virgin. The unmarried woman careth for the things of the Lord, that she may be holy both in body and in spirit: but she that is married careth for the things of the world, how she may please her husband.

*35 And this I speak for your own profit; **not that I may cast a snare upon you,** but for that which is comely, and that ye may attend upon the Lord without distraction.*

Paul says that his suggestion to remain unmarried is for their profit as regards freedom to minister, but is not binding ("cast a snare").

Answer to a Question We Know Not

36 But if any man think that he behaveth himself uncomely toward his virgin, if she pass the flower of her age, and need so require, let him do what he will, he sinneth not: let them marry.

37 Nevertheless he that standeth stedfast in his heart, having no necessity, but hath power over his own will, and hath so decreed in his heart that he will keep his virgin, doeth well.

38 So then he that giveth her in marriage doeth well; but he that giveth her not in marriage doeth better.

You can consult the commentaries to enhance your confusion over this one. It may be that this passage is not hard to understand—just hard to believe. But it is not relevant to our discussion of divorce and remarriage, so we will leave it to sleep in the pages of equally uncertain writers.

A Restatement of the Law of God concerning the Permanence of the Married State

39 The wife is bound by the law as long as her husband liveth; but if her husband be dead, she is at liberty to be married to whom she will; only in the Lord.

This everlasting principle, established at creation and affirmed by our Lord, has not lost its holiness or integrity despite the hardness of hearts and distresses brought on by people who fail to keep their marriage vows before God and man. The higher road is to honor one's vows and be faithful to that person with whom you are one flesh. And if your partner is unbelieving and does not honor the vow, putting you away, then remain unmarried or be reconciled to your spouse.

Paul's Restatement of His View of the Superiority of Celibacy

Apparently, one of the questions sent to Paul from Corinth was from a woman whose husband had left her, and she wanted to know if it was proper for her to remarry.

> *40 But she is happier if she so abide, after my judgment: and I think also that I have the Spirit of God.*

Paul Does Not Permit Remarriage for the Guilty Party in a Divorce

Paul's permissiveness does not entirely reverse what Christ said in Matthew 5 and 19. Paul said that one who has been put away (divorced, abandoned, etc.) by his/her spouse (or, the innocent party in a marriage dissolved by adultery) is not under bondage to the marriage union and may marry again without sinning, but he does not say that one who puts away one's spouse is free to marry again without committing adultery. Nor does he say that a virgin who marries the one who did the putting away is not sinning.

If you have willfully terminated your marriage on grounds other than adultery by your spouse, and you were not put away against your will, then you will still be committing adultery when you remarry. Paul says you are to remain unmarried or be reconciled. Of course, if the one you put away has remarried, there is no way you can ever be reconciled. It appears you have relegated yourself to "celibacy land" for the remainder of your life, unless you are ready to willfully sin and share that sin with your new spouse.

If you come to Christ having been the guilty party in terminating a marriage, and discover to your shame that you committed adultery when you remarried, Paul says you are to remain in the state you were in when you came to Christ. The adultery is initial, not perpetual. Your original sin of adultery is forgiven when you repent, and your marriage is now sanctified. "Brethren, let every man, wherein he is called, therein abide with God" (1 Corinthians 7:24).

Summary

The point of the entire chapter is that, for the sake of ministry, the unmarried state is to be preferred unless sexual drive necessitates otherwise. But if your natural gift of sexual drive does not allow you to contain yourself, then it is better to marry even if you have been previously divorced.

Chapter 5

God Is Divorced

God and the prophets, when communicating a divine truth, usually find a parallel in nature that suitably illustrates God's truth. The best parallel God could find to represent the relationship of Christ to his church is that of husband and wife. The church is Christ's betrothed bride. The marriage will take place at the beginning of the Millennium. God the Father's wife is Israel, but he has put her away for her adultery.

Most Christians are unaware that God represents himself as a divorced husband. He was married to Israel (Hosea 2:2; Jeremiah 3:14) but put her away because of her adultery with other nations and gods.

Jeremiah 3:20

Surely as a wife treacherously departeth from her husband, so have ye dealt treacherously with me, O house of Israel, saith the LORD.

Jeremiah 3:8

And I saw, when for all the causes whereby backsliding Israel committed adultery I had put her away, and given her a bill of divorce; yet her treacherous sister Judah feared not, but went and played the harlot also.

See also Ezekiel 23 and Hosea 3 for a thorough description of their whoredoms against God.

But though God's wife, Israel, broke the covenant and abandoned God, in Hosea 2 we read an account of God keeping his own counsel, remaining unmarried, and waiting for reconciliation to his former spouse, Israel.

Hosea 2:2, 14, 19–20

*2 Plead with your mother, plead: for **she is not my wife**, neither am I her husband: let her therefore put away her whoredoms out of her sight, and her adulteries from between her breasts;*

14 Therefore, behold, I will allure her, and bring her into the wilderness, and speak comfortably unto her.

19 And I will betroth thee unto me for ever; yea, I will betroth thee unto me in righteousness, and in judgment, and in lovingkindness, and in mercies.

20 I will even betroth thee unto me in faithfulness: and thou shalt know the LORD.

Chapter 6

Questions Asked by Readers

Question:

My church says that my husband and I are living in adultery because I cannot be married again while my first husband is alive. We divorced many years ago when I was just 23 years old and my present husband and I have six children. My first husband never married again and he has since become a Christian. Should I leave my present husband and go back to my first?

Answer:

There are some cult-like groups that have committed great abomination and defiled marriages by insisting that a man or woman in their second (or more) marriage should leave their family—spouse and children—and return to the original spouse, insisting that they are living in adultery otherwise. While God has permitted divorce and remarriage on account of hard hearts, he has never permitted a man or woman to leave a second spouse and return to the first.

That remains an abomination. Anyone who would encourage a man or woman to leave their present spouse due to a former marriage is an enemy of God.

Deuteronomy 24:1–4

1 When a man hath taken a wife, and married her, and it come to pass that she find no favour in his eyes, because he hath found some uncleanness in her: then let him write her a bill of divorcement, and give it in her hand, and send her out of his house.

2 And when she is departed out of his house, she may go and be another man's wife.

3 And if the latter husband hate her, and write her a bill of divorcement, and giveth it in her hand, and sendeth her out of his house; or if the latter husband die, which took her to be his wife;

*4 **Her former husband, which sent her away, may not take her again to be his wife, after that she is defiled; for that is abomination before the LORD:** and thou shalt not cause the land to sin, which the LORD thy God giveth thee for an inheritance.*

If it were true that second marriages are not marriages at all, and that a person remains married to their first spouse until death, and their relationship with their second spouse is an ongoing state of adultery, then Jesus missed the point, for he acknowledged that the woman at the well had indeed had "five husbands," and the man she was presently with was not her husband.

If it were true that a marriage cannot be dissolved under any circumstance other than death, then certainly a book like 1 Corinthians, filled with advice and commandments on marriage, divorce, and remarriage, would have mentioned such a doctrine, commanding them to put away their wives and return to their former husbands. But nothing of the kind is ever mentioned.

The Samaritan Woman Was Divorced

Those who suggest that the woman at the well was widowed five times and not divorced are suggesting that Jesus was doing a sort of parlor trick, like a tent evangelist trying to impress his audience with his prognostic skills, revealing irrelevant details of her life to amaze her. That's ludicrous. Jesus was convicting her of sin by revealing it to her: "For thou hast had five husbands; and he whom thou now hast is not thy husband: **in that saidst thou truly**" (John 4:18). Certainly the latter part of the statement is a revelation of her sin—she is living with a man to whom she is not married.

And in the addendum "in that saidst thou truly," Jesus commends her for her honesty in saying she had no husband. He had tested her by telling her to call her husband. She was honest about her failed marital status and her present adulterous relationship.

And the woman's response to his revelation of her past was to tell the people of the city, "Come, see a man, which told me **all things that ever I did**: is not this the Christ?" (John 4:29). She characterized what he told her as "things that I **did**." The five marriages and the one fornication were not highlights of her life; they were things she "**did**."

I am amazed at the lengths to which people will go, twisting Scripture, to justify their preferred doctrines.

Question:

I am 45 years old and have been active in my church for the past twenty years. I taught Sunday school and sometimes filled in for our former pastor when he was away. But I was divorced at the age of 24. I came to know Christ six months later, and then I married my present wife about a year after that. We recently got a new pastor and he asked me to step down from teaching because he says I have two wives and that disqualifies me from leadership. Is that true? Am I married to two women? I don't even know where my former wife is. I haven't heard from her since the divorce twenty years ago.

Answer:

I am sure your pastor got that bizarre interpretation from 1 Timothy 3:2, "A bishop then must be blameless, the husband of one wife . . ." He is assuming that a marriage is never dissolved, not for adultery (Jesus said it is) and not for abandonment (Paul said it is). That is a false assumption, for a man who commits adultery with a harlot is joined into one flesh with her, breaking the former one-flesh (marriage) union. He is also ignoring the words of Paul when he characterizes a man whose wife has put him away as "loosed from a wife."

You were loosed from your first wife, no matter who was at fault, when the two of you abandoned the relationship, and that union was dissolved when either of you had an intimate relationship with another. You are not the husband of two wives. Jesus said of the woman at the well, "Thou has had five husbands." She was not the wife of her previous husbands.

What then does it mean to be the "husband of one wife"? It is because we are so far removed from the culture of that day that some do not readily understand this passage. It was common to have more than one wife. Some had three or four at one time. Solomon had 700, not counting 300 concubines. Certainly a man with four wives would not have time to consider the needs of the church. With his forty children and four women he would be mayor of a small community and head of the war department, with enough problems to keep him fully occupied.

It is probably true that a divorced and remarried man should not be a bishop, but not for the reason that he has two wives. Paul tells us in 1 Corinthians 7 that a remarried man is going to have trouble in the flesh. I see absolutely nothing wrong with you teaching Sunday school. You could be a Bible teacher or evangelist. But it would be up to the body of believers to determine if someone with your past could effectively conduct the business of the church. How will you teach on the permanence of marriage?

A church headed by a divorced man is a church with a reduced defense against the disease of divorce.

I have known divorced and remarried pastors who have a divorce rate in their church above 50%. I hate to see a divorced and remarried man stand up and talk about how blessed his second marriage is. That sends a signal to all who are having marriage troubles that a trade-in might produce more happiness.

Question:

But doesn't Romans 7:1–3 support the concept that a woman is in a continual state of adultery with her second husband? "So then if, while her husband liveth, she be married to another man, she shall be called an adulteress . . ."

Answer:

Some, in their rush to take a stand against an awful plague of easy divorces and remarriages, fail to observe the text carefully.

Romans 7:1–3

1 Know ye not, brethren, (for I speak to them that know the law,) how that the law hath dominion over a man as long as he liveth?

*2 For the woman which **hath an husband** is bound by the law to her husband so long as he liveth; but if the husband be dead, she is loosed from the law of her husband.*

*3 So then if, while her **husband liveth**, she be married to another man, she shall be called an adulteress: but if her husband be dead, she is free from that law; so that she is no adulteress, though she be married to another man.*

Note the tense of the verb "hath" in verse 2. The verb *hath* is the third-person singular present tense of *have*. The King James is the only English Bible that accurately reflects the Greek verb tense. The passage speaks of a woman who presently has a husband. He is not a former husband. He has not put her away. She has not put him away. They are a married couple. So if while her husband lives she marries another man, she will be called an adulteress, and so she should. She is a married woman fornicating with another man.

This author recognizes that this passage does not provide for divorce and remarriage under any circumstances, not even the exception Christ referenced—adultery. It is tighter than the words of Christ in Matthew 5 and 19. Why make it say more than it does?

Now go back and read verse 3 again. I will paraphrase it: *If a woman who is married to a living husband marries another man, she will be committing adultery.*

If neither copulation nor desertion dissolves former unions, then it would be true that anyone living with a second spouse would be committing adultery. Furthermore, if Moses and Paul had not been given latitude to permit remarriage, then the woman who puts away her husband, or is put away by her husband, would indeed be committing adultery when she breaks the one-flesh union by copulating with another, as in a second marriage.

But given the exceptions Paul announced in 1 Corinthians 7, a divorced and remarried woman has only one husband—the man to whom she is presently married—and she is not living in adultery.

But the tightest argument that the woman of Romans 7 is indeed presently in a married state is that nothing else would be consistent with the analogy it makes. The very heart of these four chapters (5–8) is the doctrine that sons of Adam are married to carnal flesh that holds them in bondage to sin, and that the only release is the death of the flesh—a co-crucifixion with Christ—followed by a resurrection and a marriage to another—to Christ our new husband—after the old husband (flesh) is dead.

Human nature does not allow for a woman (the future bride of Christ) to put away her husband (carnal flesh/old man/body of sin) before crucifixion with Christ. Before one believes (comes to Christ), he is still wed to the flesh (old man/former husband), and it is only as one is baptized into Christ that the old man dies and the new man is born in resurrection with Christ to be wed to him.

So the idea that the Romans 7 woman is loosed from a husband would destroy the analogy by suggesting the impossible—that a person can disassociate himself from the old man prior to coming to Christ.

Question:

I discovered that my husband has had an affair. He says it was stupid and he will not do it again, but I am wondering if I should leave him. When he became one flesh with her, he broke our union, so am I still married to him?

Answer:

He did indeed break your union, and you have the right to leave him and marry another without sinning. But the liberty to do so is not a mandate to do so. If he is repentant and you are willing to do as Christ has done and forgive him, the marriage can be restored physically and, in time, emotionally. I suggest that you read *Created to Be His Help Meet*, and he read *Created to Need a Help Meet*.

Question:

My husband told me he had been in an affair with a woman at work for over a year, but that three months ago he ended it and fired her. I understand that he violated our union by having sex with someone else. But since then we have had sex. So even though he dissolved our flesh union, it would seem that we have now reestablished a physical union. Am I still married to him or not? Since he told me of the affair, I can't stand for him to touch me. Am I free to put him away for adultery?

Answer:

The Bible does not specify any timeline on how adultery is grounds for divorce. If an adulterous person could undo the grounds for divorce by simply copulating with his spouse before informing her of the adultery, Christ's statement in Matthew 19 and Paul's argument in 1 Corinthians 7 would have holes in them big enough to drive all of Pharaoh's armies through.

I must answer like Paul and say, "I have no commandment of the Lord, but I think I have the Spirit of God regarding this matter." Yes, when you are made aware of your husband's adultery, according to Matthew 19 you are free to put him away and be married to another. Marriage is a covenant and he violated the terms of the covenant, thereby terminating it. As Paul says, "a brother or sister is not under bondage in such cases."

However, I repeat that the liberty to put away is not a mandate to do so. If he is repentant, you should forgive him and rebuild the marriage. The trouble that will come your way through divorce will probably exceed the trouble you will have in forgiving and moving forward to restore the marriage. You are going to experience pain either way. Don't allow pride to push you to loneliness.

If there are children involved, there is no question that it will be better for you to restore the marriage, even if you feel degraded and miserable for a period of time.

But once you forgive and attempt to move forward, you are in effect reconstituting the covenant of marriage. **You will not be free to "try" reconciliation for a year and then if it doesn't work out, ditch him on grounds of his former adultery.**

Those who seek a loophole in the plan of God will find it, and the loophole will become a noose around their neck and the necks of their children. There is always the need to understand the spirit of the law and follow God's heart in the matter.

Question:

My husband has not had another woman, but he has had intimacy with other men. He wasn't like that when I married him, but he got involved in pornography and one thing led to another until . . . I don't know exactly what he has done, but has he committed adultery on me so that I am free to leave him? How could he commit adultery with a man? He says he loves me and doesn't want our marriage to end, but I just can't stand for him to touch me when I know he has been out with his boyfriend. What should I do? What does God want me to do? I feel so humiliated, but I want to please God.

Answer:

The exception clause spoken by Jesus in Matthew 19 doesn't say that only adultery dissolves the union: "And I say unto you, Whosoever shall put away his wife, except it be for **fornication** . . ." (Matthew 19:9). It says *fornication*, which covers all forms of sexual contact, whether with the opposite sex or same sex, or children, or animals, or, in the near future, virtual sex.

You are not, as Paul says, "in bondage" to your husband. He has left the marriage and broken the sacred bond. However, Paul did say it would be better for you to remain unmarried. But if you cannot contain, you may marry without sinning.

Don't be hasty. After you formalize the separation he has created, stay in contact with him and encourage him to repent and be born again. Paul said, "For what knowest thou, O wife, whether thou shalt save thy husband?" (1 Corinthians 7:16[a]).

Get my video series *The Science of Addiction and the Brain* and encourage him to view it. It is yet possible to have a glorious marriage with this girly man. But before you take him back, be sure to get both of you tested for HIV and other STDs.

Question:

I was a young Christian when I divorced my wife. It was my fault. She didn't want the divorce, but at the time my life was so messed up, I made her miserable, so the marriage was indeed unhappy. I have since rededicated my life to the Lord and I want to do the right thing. Since I was a Christian when I divorced, it appears I committed adultery by remarrying. What do I do now? Am I committing adultery every time I have intimacy with my wife?

Answer:

Your marriage status has nothing to do with whether you were or were not a Christian at the time of your divorce. The institution of marriage precedes the Law and Christianity.

Christian or not, those who initiated divorce in the past and now find themselves remarried, did indeed commit adultery when they initially copulated with their new spouse. But they are not now living in ongoing adultery as some assert. To claim that they are is based on the faulty assumption that the new union did not dissolve the former. That would mean that they are either one flesh with two people—which is an oxymoron—or the new union does not, in fact, establish a union at all, and they remain one flesh with their original spouse—an emphatic contradiction of Jesus's words.

Question:

When my wife and I met we were both married to someone else. We started having an affair and eventually divorced and then married each other. We know we did wrong and have suffered in the flesh as Paul says. God has forgiven us. We even went back and asked our former spouses to forgive us. Our church has accepted us as redeemed sinners saved by grace, but there are some in our church who think we are living in sin. They don't say anything, but I can feel their condemnation. What can I do to convince them we are sorry and have been forgiven?

Answer:

God hates divorce. Most Christians do as well. You did sin. God has forgiven you, and you are no longer in sin. You are as cleansed of your sin as a newborn baby. Just as you have had weakness in the flesh, others have weakness in the spirit.

Many Christians, out of a desire to not normalize sin, feel they should maintain a distance from the soiled sinner as a signal to their children and anyone else who might be tempted to go down the same road. Weaker Christians feel the need to insulate themselves against any undue influences.

And remember, Paul did warn that you would have trouble in the flesh. Welcome to the trouble. It is your burden to bear. So bear it with grace and humility, and don't be bitter against those who condemn you. They are suffering more than you are. It is much easier emotionally if you move away and start your lives all over where people do not know you. You will be accepted as you are and not judged for what you were.

Romans 8:34

Who is he that condemneth? It is Christ that died, yea rather, that is risen again, who is even at the right hand of God, who also maketh intercession for us.

Question:

My husband is an insufferable, selfish, angry man. He is narcissistic and has control issues. I do not believe in divorce, so I have refused to be intimate with him. He sleeps in the den, and has done so for over a year now. I am sure he is viewing pornography in his late nights with his computer. He doesn't believe like I do, so I am sure he is going to divorce me. I would not think of divorcing him, and I would not think of marrying another man as long as we are married before God. Will I be free to marry again after he commits fornication in marrying someone else?

Answer:

You are seeking to take advantage of what you think is a loophole in the words of Jesus in Matthew 19. A woman could starve her husband out sexually and emotionally, driving him away, then wait for him to remarry—committing adultery—and then she would be free to marry as the victim who did not commit adultery. Paul demolished that possibility by telling us that putting away a spouse makes you the guilty party. He may marry without sinning because you "put him away" even as you lived in the same house with him and refused to be his wife in the biblical sense. But when you remarry you will be committing adultery, not he.

"This legal institution of
a **state-regulated marriage**
may have its benefits,
but it is not recognized by God as
holy matrimony."

Chapter 7

Licensed to Marry?

Who has the authority to permit a couple to enter into holy matrimony? Presently, all but nine states say only the state has the power to create a marriage. A license is a permit—permission. The issuer of licenses lays down the terms, authorizes the marriage, and issues a license to the one who performs the ceremony. The licensing of a thing assumes it is not legal unless the license is obtained. A license also assumes the continuing jurisdiction of the one granting the license.

The Value of a Legal Marriage Document

There was a time when the church performed and recorded the weddings. If a couple wanted a divorce 150 years ago, they had to go to the church and justify the dissolution of a covenant to which they had sworn. The divorce rate was less than 3%. As the world became more secularized and economically complex, the church allowed the state to assume jurisdiction over marriages. In our modern world controlled by finances, property, and permits, the state is able to arbitrate according to law. A state marriage license creates something like a mini corporation. Each member—husband and wife—assumes legal liability. Banking, taxes, the payment of debts, parental rights and duties, etc., are shared by husband and wife. If a man dies, the state-recognized wife receives all his property. Otherwise she has no claim over inheritance. Likewise, the legal status of children, the right to a say-so in emergency medical procedures, etc., are shared by the state-married couple. A legal spouse has certain privileges in regard to her husband if he is hospitalized. On the other hand, if the man defaults on a debt, the wife is liable (in some states, but not all).

There is obviously a temporal benefit in "incorporating" a marriage by means of seeking and receiving a license from the state to be married, for it is a contractual agreement that grants jurisdiction to the state and enables each person to appeal to the court for the enforcement of his/her rights should it become necessary.

Holy Matrimony

This legal institution of a state-regulated marriage may have its benefits, but it is not recognized by God as holy matrimony. If it were, then God would be bound by the parameters and dictates of the state. Same-sex marriage, which carries all the judicial authority of a traditional marriage, would now be "what God hath joined together"—a ridiculous absurdity. Likewise, when the state grants a divorce on grounds not acceptable to God, then God would have to honor it. How asinine! If the state is the determiner of marriage, then get ready for a man to have four wives and a woman to marry her dog, because that is where the state is headed.

It is time to stop saying "marriage" and start speaking of "holy matrimony." That is a place the state cannot go—dare not go. It is well past time for the church to assume sole jurisdiction over holy matrimony and tell the state it can keep its marriage laws and do with them as it pleases. Tell the state we do not seek its approval and we do not accept its jurisdiction over our holy matrimony.

If God does not recognize a state-licensed marriage, is that to say that having gone that route, I am not married? Not at all. Holy matrimony can take place at the same time as a state marriage. When a couple makes a culturally appropriate public commitment to enter into holy matrimony and they consummate that union, God has joined them together no matter what the state does or does not do.

A legal divorce by the state does not end holy matrimony. Holy matrimony ends at death or when one spouse puts the other away—for whatever reason.

Bigamy

Since it will probably be in the news by the time this book is published, we will discuss bigamy. A "one-flesh" union is composed of one man and one woman. A man cannot be one flesh with two women at the same time. It is contrary to nature. I go on record now because in five to ten years when the Supreme Court discovers that it is "a right afforded us by the Constitution," bigamy will become popular in some Christian circles, and it will be a topic of debate throughout the church.

The Scriptures say you are to love your wife as you love yourself. Taking a second wife is a statement that the first one is not enough for you. How would you feel if your wife decided she needed two husbands? Or three? Or four? You would get your turn to ride shotgun, but part of the time you would have to sit in the back seat and be happy. No woman feels cherished who is not elevated to the one-and-only status. There can be only one queen in the hive.

Chapter 8

Reflection

A Plague of Hard Hearts

If the hearts of men and women were hard in the days of Moses and there was distress in the early church over marriage, today we are swallowed up by a plague of hard hearts and self-pleasing hedonists jumping from one marriage to the next, and one relationship to two more while the first one is winding down. In 1879 the divorce rate was 3%. In 1900 it was 7%. In 1958 it was 21%. In 1970 no-fault divorce was made available, and by 1980 the divorce rate was 52%. Statistics show that of those getting married today, 50% or more will get divorced. The divorce rate has not continued to climb for the simple reason that those couples who know they are not prepared to make a lifetime commitment are not getting married. They just perpetually fornicate, moving from one partner to another.

Christian Divorce Rate

Some have claimed that evangelical Christians have a higher divorce rate than the nation as a whole. That is propaganda put out by those who want to denigrate God's people. Harvard-trained researcher Shaunti Feldhahn did an eight-year study and determined that the divorce rate among evangelical Christians was about 15% to 20%. In some circles it was less than 10%. So being a Christian does make a difference, but the rate is still too high. I do think that with so many Christian men, and more than a few women, turning to pornography, in ten years we will see a significant increase in the divorce rate among Christians.

Spirit-filled Christians shouldn't settle for God's permissive will, accepting divorce as an alternative in their quest for personal fulfilment. Men should learn to be the savior of their wives, and women should learn to be help meets to their husbands. When we stand before God and man and enter into a covenant "until death do us part," there can be no reason to choose to back out of it except adultery or abandonment.

Christian Bigots

It is understandable to hate divorce. God does. Those of us who have to deal with the aftermath in so many lives know the evils firsthand.

But there is another plague bringing great harm to the church. It is borne in the hearts of those who have never been divorced and are certain they will

THE BIBLE ON DIVORCE AND REMARRIAGE | MICHAEL PEARL

never be. Some fall into sin, and others fall into condemnation of the brethren. The church is biting and devouring itself (Galatians 5:15). It is being consumed from within, like an autoimmune disease in which the body attacks itself, slowly weakening until it can no longer resist attacks from without.

Where is the mercy, grace, and humility of Christ in the church today? Snootiness toward the fallen is not an expression of righteousness; it is pride that leads to destruction.

Many people find it difficult to live their convictions unless they are controlling those who differ with them. They have the need to express negative feelings toward those more sinful than themselves so as to provide insulation against any undue influences. What they call taking a stand is more than standing in the light; it is standing over those who have fallen down. They call it letting their light shine, but they spend their energy shining their bright light in the eyes of others. And they accuse everyone who doesn't join them in their crusade against "sinners" of being "soft on sin."

The mark of Christian bigots is a lack of joy. They are distinctly devoid of forgiveness, praise, worship, and joy.

More Righteous Than God

If we are open to the words of God, even though they offend our natural sense of righteousness, we must acknowledge that those in their second or third . . . or

81

even fifth marriage are not living in adultery. They have enough problems in the flesh without having to kneel in shame before their many "Christian" accusers. The Bible records Jesus's rebuke of a number of sins, but he never rebuked a remarried person as one living in adultery. And of all the New Testament epistles filled with repeated denunciation of various sins of the church, not once do any of the writers rebuke the church for having married couples living in a state of adultery. If such a doctrine were true, it would have been a glaring oversight for the writers to not address it.

As Paul said, "Let every man abide in the same calling wherein he was called" (1 Corinthians 7:20). There is no going back. Move forward from where you are, and live in the grace and forgiveness of Christ.

Chapter 9

How to Relate to Divorces in the Church

Divorce is the tragic result of broken humanity living undisciplined, selfish lives. Whenever a marriage fails, we should mourn it as tragic. But there should be no error against the marriage so grave that it cannot be forgiven where there is repentance. A crime against children or wife is a different matter, but no sin against the marriage is beyond the reach of grace.

In a day when all moral standards are falling to promiscuous ideologies, those of us who want to hold to biblical standards find it increasingly difficult to surround ourselves with a hedge of morality. We have lost control of our nation, our communities, our churches, and even our homes. Most Christians can't even control themselves.

The few upright souls that live disciplined lives do indeed vex their righteous souls on a daily basis with the ungodly deeds surrounding them (2 Peter 2:8–9).

The Biblical Response

The biblical principle is that divorce and remarriage are not permitted except for adultery or desertion, and that is the rule the church should promote. Ministers and teachers should make young people aware that marriage is for life—until death—and not something to be cast aside when one feels unfulfilled.

When a church member willfully terminates their marriage on any ground other than adultery or desertion, the church should expect the guilty party to remain unmarried. If the guilty party does remarry, s/he should be subjected to the discipline of the church and be required to publicly express repentance, asking God and the church for forgiveness. If they are unwilling to do so, they should be put out of the assembly (Matthew 18:17).

There is no justification given in the Bible for divorce on grounds of incompatibility, lack of love, or differing career goals. It is not feasible that two born-again Christians who are dedicated to serving Jesus Christ should not be able to maintain their marriage and see it grow into something beautiful.

If your marriage history is sordid and ugly, do not fail to access the grace of God. There is a fountain open for sin and uncleanness. All who come are welcomed, and all who receive unmerited forgiveness are crowned with mercy and grace.

Accept God's forgiveness, ignore the Christian bigots, and enjoy your present marriage no matter how it came to be. Look forward—not back—

and live the life you now have to the glory of God without recrimination.

Personal Note

The views found in this book are not unique. I have been teaching this subject in the same manner for fifty years, as attested to by my earlier audio messages on 1 Corinthians.

At No Greater Joy Ministries we have received literally thousands of letters that could be answered by this book. I have waited so long to put it in book form because other subjects seemed so much more important. And, frankly, I hate divorce. I have never officiated at a wedding involving a previously married individual whose former spouse was still alive. It is not out of conviction that I have not participated; it just makes me uncomfortable. In my thinking, a holy matrimony ceremony should be a celebration of something perfect.

I don't offer these thoughts as a suggestion as to how one should view remarriage. It may be my bigoted weakness that causes me to be so standoffish. The reason I confess my weakness in regard to something Paul says is not sin, but is allowed only because of the hardness of hearts, is that I think many of my "one-time married" friends feel the same way. And I think that attitude is at the root of much of the resistance to the words of Paul concerning remarriage. That deep feeling of discomfort—that remarriage after divorce is just not in the natural order—

motivates us to withdraw from those who have failed in their marriages.

Now, the question I have had to face and the challenge I put before you is this: do I have the right to judge others whom God has suffered to do what is not his perfect will? If I reject the present marriage of the formerly divorced, am I not also rejecting the grace of God and judging God for allowing that which makes me uncomfortable? Are my feelings above the words of God as recorded in 1 Corinthians 7?

Some will charge, and perhaps rightly so, that widely published acknowledgement of the sanctity of remarried couples will tear down the walls of resistance and encourage more divorces. But who are we to build fences where God has not? Paul said "a brother or sister is **not under bondage** in such cases." Are we to erect walls of ostracism and criticism for the purpose of creating fear in others who might be contemplating ending their miserable marriages? Remember, those who willfully end their marriages are not free to remarry without committing adultery. But should we put in bondage those innocent parties in a divorce to whom God has given a reprieve?

The temptation to push God aside and take his place on the throne of judgment is probably more pressing here than on any other issue. A little humility is in order.

Finally, I know that with the publication of this book I will lose the favor of some. I regret that. But I have never been moved by what others think or how they might respond if I tell them the truth. At 70 years old, this one-time-married Bible teacher is not going to seek popularity with men over faithfulness to the words of God.

I am open to any intelligent and well-informed critique of this work. If you can show me where I have interpreted the words of God incorrectly, I will print a retraction. But if you change the words of God to make your point, you will have no basis of discussing anything other than your attack upon the perfect Word of God.

"Here I stand; I cannot do otherwise."

—Martin Luther

" Though I *speak* with the tongues
of men <u>and</u> of angels,
and *have not* *charity*,
I am become as *sounding brass*,
or a *tinkling cymbal.*

And though I have the gift
of **prophecy**, and understand
all mysteries, and <u>all knowledge</u>;
and though I have <u>all faith</u>,
so that I could *remove mountains,*
and have not **charity**,
I am *nothing*.

And though I bestow **all my goods**
<u>to feed the poor</u>, and though
I give my body to be burned,
and have not *charity*,
it profiteth me nothing.

Charity <u>suffereth long</u>,
and is *kind*;
charity <u>envieth *not*</u>;
charity <u>vaunteth *not* itself</u>,
is <u>*not* puffed up</u>,

Doth <u>not</u> **behave** itself *unseemly,*
seeketh <u>not</u> her own, is <u>not</u> easily
provoked, thinketh <u>no evil</u>;

Rejoiceth <u>not</u> in iniquity,
but **rejoiceth in the** *truth*;

Beareth all things, *believeth* all things,
hopeth all things, **endureth <u>all things</u>**.

Charity *never* faileth:

but whether there be **prophecies**,
they <u>shall</u> *fail*; whether there be
tongues, they <u>shall</u> *cease*;
whether there be **knowledge**,
it <u>shall</u> *vanish away*.

For we *know* <u>in part</u>,
and we *prophesy* <u>in part</u>.

But when that which is *perfect*
is come, then that which is
<u>in part</u> shall be **done away.**

When I was a **child**, I *spake* as
a **child**, I *understood* as a **child**,
I *thought* as a **child**:
but when I became a *man*,
I <u>put away</u> *childish* things.

For now we see *through a glass*,
<u>darkly</u>; but then **<u>face to face</u>**:
now I know in part; but **then** shall I
know even as also I *am known*.

And now abideth **faith**, **hope**,
charity, these three; but the
<u>greatest</u> of these is *charity*. ”

1 Corinthians 13

Marriage Resources

For more material published by NGJ, including books and videos on child training, downloadable audio teachings on Bible topics, homeschooling resources and much more, visit our website at www.nogreaterjoy.org or call toll-free, 866-292-9936.

Volume discounts are available on many items. We also offer a Distributorship Program for churches and resellers. Call for more info.

For Men

Created to Need a Help Meet

Men know they need their wives sexually, but most don't know they need their wives emotionally, spiritually, and mentally in order to be well-rounded, thoughtful, balanced, and motivated men. You'll be a better man once you come to see the whole truth. Men, this book is for you. Also available as an audio book. By Michael Pearl. 245 pages.

In Search of a Help Meet

Choosing your life's partner is one of the most important and life-directing decisions you'll ever make. This book may save you from making the biggest mistake of your life. Also available as an audio book. By Michael & Debi Pearl. 250 pages.

Becoming a Man

This message is for parents concerned about raising their boys up to be men and it is for fathers who never learned to be real men. By Michael Pearl. Audio CD, 35 min.

Only Men

Michael Pearl speaks directly and frankly to men about their responsibilities as husbands. By Michael Pearl. Audio CD, 74 min. *Also available in Spanish.*

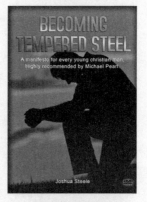

Becoming Tempered Steel

As a young teenager Joshua Steele dedicated his life to serving God and has followed his calling with the force of tempered steel. He came to Cane Creek and addressed the young men on the subject of moral purity and preparation to serve God. By Joshua Steele. 135 min.

Pornography: Road to Hell

Most ministers avoid the subject, but Michael shows how repentance toward God and the power of the gospel of Jesus Christ can break the bondage of this wicked perversion through the abundant mercy and grace of a loving God. By Michael Pearl. 12 pages. *Also available in Spanish.*

For Women

Created to Be His Help Meet

Discover how God can make your marriage glorious! What God is doing through this book is amazing. We've received thousands of letters from wives and husbands giving testimony to marriages restored and old loves rekindled. Also available as an audio book. By Debi Pearl. 336 pages. *Also available in Spanish.*

The Help Meet's Journey

The Journey is a year-long companion workbook/journal for Created to Be His Help Meet. There are extra pages for your stories, doodlings, and studies. By Debi Pearl. 184 pages.

Preparing to Be a Help Meet

Being a good help meet starts long before marriage. It is a mindset, a learned habit, a way of life established as a young unmarried girl. A perfect study guide for small groups. Also available as an audio book. By Debi Pearl. 296 pages. *Also available in Spanish.*

For Both Men & Women

Marriage God's Way

Husbands, learn how to sanctify your wife and cleanse her of spots, wrinkles, and blemishes. You have the power to bring your wife into the fullness of all that God intended her to be. Wives, learn the freedom of honoring and ministering to your man. Help him become all that God intended him to be. By Michael Pearl. 2-DVD set, 184 min.

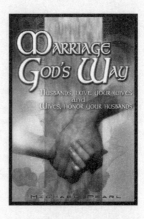

Holy Sex: Song of Solomon

A refreshing journey through biblical texts showing that God designed marriage to be the context of erotic pleasure. By Michael Pearl. 82 pages. *Also available in Spanish.*

Science of Addiction and the Brain

Addiction is the state of being enslaved to a substance or habit. At the 2014 Shindig, Michael delivered four packed messages supported by 185 animated PowerPoint slides on this subject. By Michael Pearl. 1 DVD, 222 min.

To Betroth
or Not to Betroth

All Christian parents want their
children to have God's first and
best in all areas of their lives,
and this includes marriage. In an
effort to avoid the dangers of the
modern dating game, families are
giving attention to the concept
of betrothal. The dangers of the
betrothal system are exposed with
biblical truth, bringing objectivity
back to an often-misunderstood subject.
By Michael Pearl. 28 pages.

Young Adults & Marriage

The first crop of homeschoolers
are either married or ready for
marriage. This message, taught
by Michael Pearl in California,
was given to help parents and
their young adult children make
wise decisions. It has the story of
all five of his children finding their mates. It should prove
entertaining. By Michael Pearl. Audio CD, 54 min.

By Divine Design

If you are philosophically
minded, this book will appeal to
you. It addresses the question,
"Why, God, did you let this
happen?" By Michael Pearl.
85 pages.

"**Blessed** is the man that walketh not
in the counsel of the ungodly,
nor standeth in the way of sinners,
nor sitteth in the seat of the scornful.
But his *delight* is in the law
of the LORD; and in his law
doth he meditate day and night.

And he shall be like a **tree**
planted by the rivers of water,
that bringeth forth his fruit
in his season;
his leaf also shall not wither; and
whatsoever he doeth shall **prosper**.

The ungodly are not so:
but are like the chaff
which the wind driveth away.

Therefore the ungodly **shall not
stand** in the judgment, nor sinners
in the congregation of the righteous.
For the LORD *knoweth*
the way of the **righteous**:
but the way of the ungodly shall perish."

Psalm 1